Bumper Stickers on the Clouds

Humor and Essays from an Uncommon Christian

RON RITTS

WestBow
PRESS

A DIVISION OF THOMAS NELSON

Scriptures taken from the Holy Bible, New International Version®, NIV®.
Copyright © 1973, 1978, 1984, 2011 by Biblica, Inc.™ Used by permission
of Zondervan. All rights reserved worldwide. www.zondervan.com The
"NIV" and "New International Version" are trademarks registered in
the United States Patent and Trademark Office by Biblica, Inc.™

WestBow Press books may be ordered through booksellers or by contacting:

WestBow Press
A Division of Thomas Nelson
1663 Liberty Drive
Bloomington, IN 47403
www.westbowpress.com
1 (866) 928-1240

Because of the dynamic nature of the Internet, any web addresses or
links contained in this book may have changed since publication and
may no longer be valid. The views expressed in this work are solely those
of the author and do not necessarily reflect the views of the publisher,
and the publisher hereby disclaims any responsibility for them.

Any people depicted in stock imagery provided by Thinkstock are models,
and such images are being used for illustrative purposes only.
Certain stock imagery © Thinkstock.

ISBN: 978-1-4908-1849-8 (sc)
ISBN: 978-1-4908-1850-4 (hc)
ISBN: 978-1-4908-1848-1 (e)

Library of Congress Control Number: 2013922048

Printed in the United States of America.

WestBow Press rev. date: 12/27/2013

CONTENTS

DEDICATION

This book was written for all the people who believe that it is our God-given right to laugh, think, and think when we laugh.

Being a Christian is a life-long occupation. We never stop learning and we never stop getting better at becoming closer to God. But, as in the earthly life itself, we must always study, practice, learn from others, and serve a purpose.

Hopefully this book will make you think! The rewards of living as a Christian are fully resolved in the Everlasting, not in the earthly context!

PREFACE

Quite often, I have found that humor is a good way to get the attention of many people. It enables them to laugh, smile, relax, and feel at ease. Humor can also be used as an extension of the Christian Life to bring The Word to more people and challenge them to think about what they are reading or hearing. The following pages will revive memories, present some new thoughts, and make you smile.

This body of work contains notes and writings from many years of just "jotting things down." There are those things that pop into your mind like an inspiration from God, but then, as you develop the idea, you begin to wonder "Why would I think of such a thing?" Finally, I had so many items amassed that God presented what His plan was all along: use them to bring the importance of The Word to others. Use the writings to both amuse and to remind all Christians (or potential Christians) of the confirmation and conviction needed to attain Eternity with Him.

I know that Christians today are dedicated to the church and to God's service, but may also get tied up in their own emotions and opinions in many church functions or meetings. For instance, belonging to a church committee and attempting to decide how many committees it takes to change a light bulb. Or who should change the bulb. Or what committee decides how bright it should be. Or "How are we going to pay for it?"

Please always remember to be joyful in your Christian Faith. Our complicated and busy lives also compete with our Faith values and Faith time. Many situations we find ourselves in can result in a myriad of emotions: up, down, happy, sad, depressed, angry, and on and on. But always Be Joyful and Trust God.

Acknowledgement - Gracious and Glorious Thanks

I would like to thank all who contributed to the writing of this book.

Praise and Thanks to God for finally saying "GO", and for Being.

Thank you to Jesus for always being by my side and providing the superb material for the basis of most of my subject matter.

Thank you to the Holy Spirit for support, inspiration, and motivation.

Thank you to my very loving and very patient wife, who for over forty years has supported me in everything I do. I am still falling in love with her, despite the dozens, no hundreds of eye-rolls and head-shakes she has given me through the years. She was thrilled to accept God's proposition of my call to work "full time" as an author and speaker. Her support continues to energize and motivate me.

Thank you to my Immediate Family.

Thank you to my Extended Family.

Thank you to my Extended Church Family.

Thank you to my Newly Extended Christian Family.

INTRODUCTION
- SUGGESTIONS FOR
READING THIS BOOK

Recently, we have found in this country that humor can be offensive. In fact, it is now believed by some that ALL humor is offensive and should be banned completely.

I was on the street the other day, and made eye contact with a man that looked like he wanted to hear a joke. So I said to him. "Knock, Knock!"

He responded, "I suppose YOU thought that was funny. You should know I'm homeless and am offended by the jokes that make fun of my situation!"

In reading this book, please remember that God gave us a sense of humor. My humor may be termed "unusual", but it is the strongest of the talents that I have. (Sigh.)

The sometimes humorous writings within these pages are to help you realize that God wants us to be our very best and serve Him with our talents and gifts, but also to serve Him happily, and without embarrassment or remorse. The brief essays included hopefully will express my hope for each of you to live more complete Christian lives.

While reading this book, you will notice that it skips around a lot. Scriptures in this collection are random, as far as any singular or progression of topic goes. This is intentional to the extent that my thoughts tend to skip around a lot. But that's the way life is, unless you are not into skipping.

As a Christian, my references to Bible passages tend to be from the New Testament. I also have attempted to cite many of the stories in the Old Testament, which give us a pretty clear picture of just how omnipotent God is. But, God willing, I will be able to write much more in the near future covering other subjects and scripture.

Now, please let me continue. There is a "small" selection of the subjects of humor and jokes that have been found to be offensive; a brief but incomplete list follows. We have the –ist category: sexist, racist, ageist, off color-ist. Then there are the opposite categories: skinny/fat, rich/poor, smart/stupid, and religion/atheist. And the pro-anti categories: government, fame, marriage, homosexual, social status, education, sanity, health, ethics, states, countries, animals, people, and aliens.

Puns are offensive to the English language as well as to the people who groan when they hear them. Satire is usually stupid and makes fun of whatever it is referring to, but much of it is also hysterical. Slapstick is offensive to anyone who has had someone laugh at them when they have had an accident, but it still looks really funny.

If you look hard enough, all humor and jokes could be considered offensive to someone, something, or anything.

I believe that most humor is funny, and probably there is still a lot of it that I just don't get. But we need laughter to live. A doctor somewhere said that, so it must be true. There is even laughter therapy to help people cope with everyday life, and that just makes me sad.

Humor is God's gift to all: it helps them to relieve stress, relax, and enjoy life, and give us hope that all is not lost. Let the laughter in your life be contagious to others!

BUMPER STICKERS
ON THE CLOUDS

Have you seen them?

The following bumper stickers have been seen on God's clouds, and He puts them there for us to see and be reminded of His need for us to remember His love. You may have missed a lot of these if you haven't been watching closely.

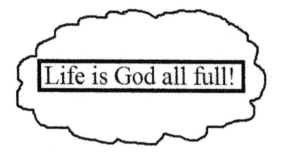

Wonderful Counselor, Almighty
Father, Prince of Peace,
The Way, Alpha and Omega,
Immanuel, Lord, Holy Spirit,
The Son Jesus, Jehovah,
Abba, Bread of Life.
Just call Me God for short.

Nobody is My co-pilot!

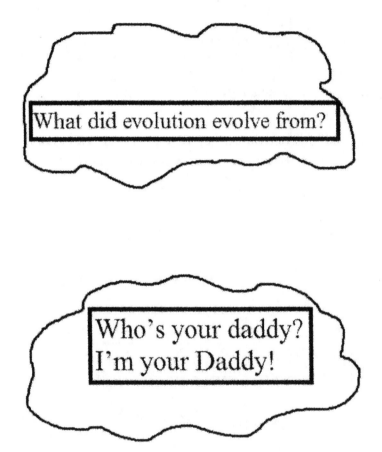

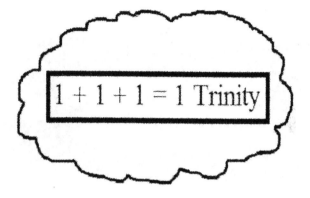

1 + 1 + 1 = 1 Trinity

A rolling stone gathers no moss,
but it does open the tomb.

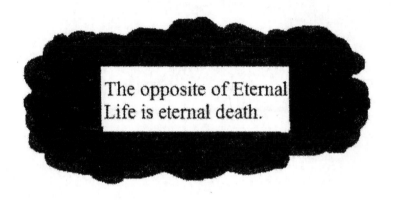

The opposite of Eternal Life is eternal death.

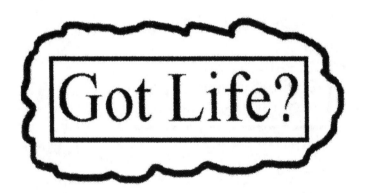

Got Life?

To get to Heaven, follow the signs and obey the laws.

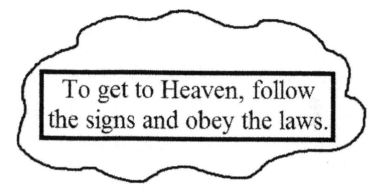

If a tree falls in the forest and no one is there, do I hear it? YES!

Some of My best work is here in the sky
—beautifully shaped clouds, breathtaking
sunsets, powerful lightening, and
awesome rainbows.

If you are close
enough to read this,
then get closer to Me.

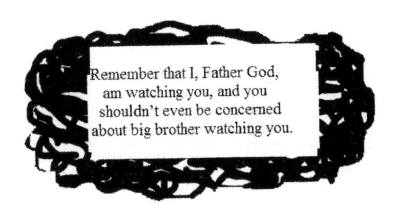

Remember that I, Father God,
am watching you, and you
shouldn't even be concerned
about big brother watching you.

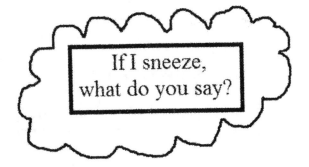

If I sneeze,
what do you say?

You are looking at Evolution
as Created by God.

Eternal Life:
To Death and Beyond!

Eternal Life isn't for everybody.
Many people just don't get it.

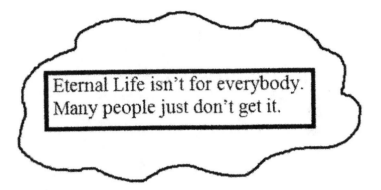

I don't just bless the citizens
of the U.S. of America; I bless
Christians all over the world!

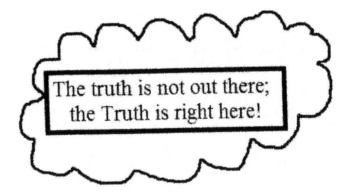

I have a Son named Jesus,
but I do not have a daughter
named Mother Nature.
She is an Angel that I assigned to
watch over the seasons, the
flora and fauna of the earth.

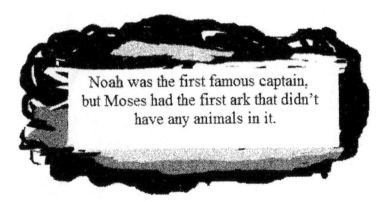

Noah was the first famous captain,
but Moses had the first ark that didn't
have any animals in it.

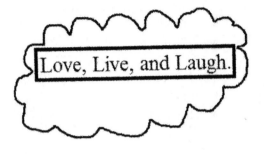

Love, Live, and Laugh.

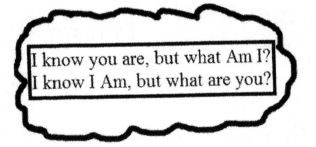

I know you are, but what Am I?
I know I Am, but what are you?

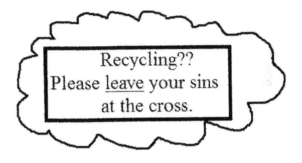

Recycling??
Please <u>leave</u> your sins
at the cross.

Where are the apostles
when you need them?

Do not pass.
Stop and believe!
Then go and sin no more.

Heaven or hell;
it's not a 50 – 50 chance
of one or the other.

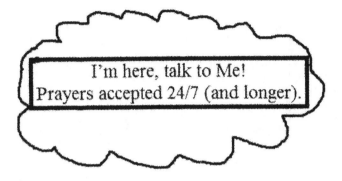

I'm here, talk to Me!
Prayers accepted 24/7 (and longer).

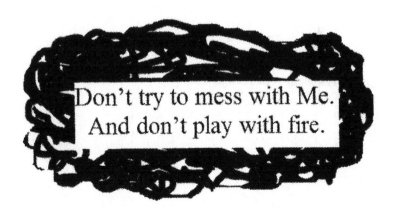

Don't try to mess with Me.
And don't play with fire.

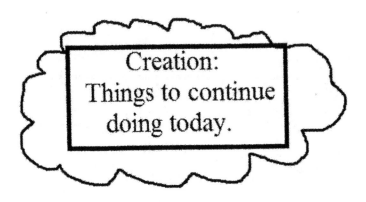

Creation:
Things to continue
doing today.

My other cloud is an all electric cloud.
I'm conserving My energy
for better things.

My Son is an Honor Student at The
Right Hand Academy of God.

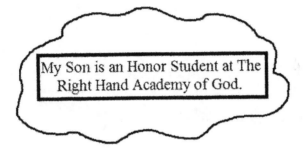

The Trinity is
My (W)hole in one!

Some fishermen catch fish.
Real Fishermen are Christians
who "fish" for those who would
become Christians.

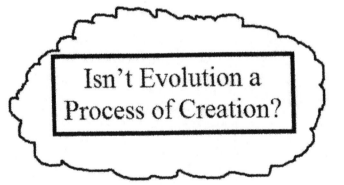

Isn't Evolution a
Process of Creation?

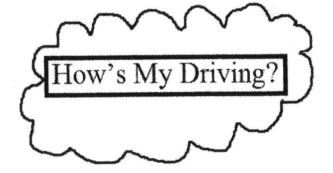

CREATION

Universal Limitations

What is it about the universe these days?

In recent years, there have been several reports about the universe shrinking and /or growing. In addition, there are also reports of locating the edge of the universe and estimations of the size and shape of the universe.

If we get to the edge of the universe, do we fall off? Please Christopher Columbus, please turn the ship around before that happens!

The universe is never-ending! It's the UNIVERSE! It is not shrinking, growing, or limited to boundaries. I even read where a scientist believes that there are probably universes beyond ours. Even a referral to the "known universe" does not make sense, by definition.

Creavolution – Pronounced "crea" (as in create, with a long "a" sound) – "volution" (as in evolution.) As described in Genesis, this is the process of the creation of the earth along with the rest of the universe. God also made sure that there were plenty of questions unanswered, so that some of us would spend our entire lives trying to get to the bottom of the beginning of the universe by promoting "theories" about a "big bang" or tear apart atoms until the "God particle" is found.

"In the beginning" is actually, then "in the middle" because God was, is, and always will be. God knows the past, the present, and the future. Research in space and on the earth continues to supply us with new and unimaginable data, and the sciences have discovered many things. With all of this knowledge, though, we discover only processes and causal events. The ultimate question which still persists is the "why". Why do any of these events occur at all? Is it because it is the order and laws of the universe? Why are there laws and order and not just chaos? If there is chaos, why does order exist in some areas and not others? Why do I have a cold in the summertime?

Technology still cannot attain the quality of a direct and immediate connection to the internet that compares to the direct connection you can make with God by just bowing your head.

Roses, squirrels, and birds, oh my! I can see these things as I write sometimes, because we have a very comfortable screened–in back porch on our house. The very details in each of these creations are equally amazing and fascinating. They are both wonderful and entertaining to look at as they each do their own thing. (Yes, in their own way, roses are definitely entertaining.) God cares for everything on the planet, and hopes that we can be successful caretakers of the earth. God has also made the universe with specific scientific laws and events that keep it in auto-pilot mode. But there are little miracles (or as some say, coincidences) that occur each day which seem to contradict these laws. Someone found alive in a catastrophic accident, the complete unexplained cure of a disease that should have been fatal, the car accident that almost happened, or the glass bowl that I just dropped on the floor that didn't shatter into a million pieces and get me into trouble because it is one of my wife's favorite bowls.

Man and Woman

It Must Have Been Something I Ate

Did you hear about the guy who got caught using colorful language? He got sent to prism!

Are you aware of the difference between the colors in the arch of a rainbow and the spectrum of colors that a prism produces? A prism can break light into the colors which make up light, commonly known as Roy G. Biv. At least the spectrum is known to some of us as Roy G. Biv. The prism, when the light and prism are set up correctly, spreads the colors in a straight line in the order of Roy's name. For the forgetful, inquisitive, or people who don't know Roy, the letters in order stand for: red, orange, yellow, green, blue, indigo, violet.

Rainbows are different, but of course similar. Although the colors are evident to the human eye, they are not only bent into an arch, but also blended or blurred as one color goes into the next. Notably, this is because the rain which is creating the colors is not a flat-sided prism, but made up of curved droplets of water which bend the spectrum into a remarkable arch across the sky. Experts claim that because of the blending and bending, some of the seven colors of the spectrum cannot be seen. Also, the background may have an effect in hiding some of the colors.

I must say that this may or may not be true. For at least two times in my life, I have seen Roy G. Biv in a rainbow, and I mean all of him. Thank you God.

Quoted from Genesis 1:31: "God saw all that He had made, and it was very good. And there was evening, and there was morning - the sixth day."

And 2:3: "And God blessed the seventh day and made it holy, because on it He rested from all the work of creating that He had done."

(Note: not an actual verse.) And as God rested and reflected upon His creation, He thought to Himself, "I created man and woman. I probably shouldn't have created them exactly in My image, because they won't be able to handle it. Maybe next time I'll do it differently!"

The woman took some (of the apple) and ate it; and also gave some to her husband, and he ate it. They hid from the Lord God among the trees in the garden. Adam said, "I heard You in the garden and I was afraid because I was naked; so I hid." (Paraphrased, kind of, from Genesis 3: 6-12.)

And God said, "Good one Adam! You people crack Me up! Who were you hiding from, Me or each other?"

Hence, the true evidence of God's humor began in the book of Genesis solely due to the existence of mankind – Adam and Eve, to be exact. Okay, God had already played a couple of practical jokes on a few animals (the duckbill platypus, the giraffe, the dung beetle, and the anteater, to name a few), but the legacy of humor was bestowed upon the man and woman so that they would get it too.

Of course, in the above instance, being the fall guys of the joke, Adam and Eve weren't really trying to be funny. But Adam's first reaction is "She did it! It's her fault!", and Eve's retort is "Nuh-uh, the snake told me that it was okay!" You can picture it as each one pointed to their accused as they said it. But God got it. Even though

He knew it was coming, it was still funny the way that it happened. From there on out, the humor of God and mankind has been present all over the world, in every society and race, and in every country and economic class.

Personkind (mankind + womankind) is the only segment of God's creation, it is said, that can laugh and weep. And, just to be funny, we can shed tears doing both. Some say that hyenas laugh, but they don't really think anything is funny, and when they do make sounds, it's usually not a good sign for some other animal. I know that my cats laugh at me on the inside because of what they have trained me to do for them, but no one can prove it. And dogs look like they laugh when they pant, but you can tell that they really don't get it because when you tell them a joke, they quit panting and just stare at you, even if it's a very funny joke.

If you haven't figured it out by now, God always has the last laugh. We can be amazed and wonder about some of God's creations, but we find it hard to laugh when all we have to do is look at our own bodies in the mirror. Yeah, He let us eat from the tree of knowledge, but since we need to clothe ourselves now, He made our bodies so that nothing would fit right. If evolution were true, wouldn't our bodies have adapted by now to the structure where our shoulders are squared off so that our shirts would only need hospital corner folds to make them fit right?

But I digress. God's sense of humor is probably not like yours and most assuredly is not like mine. He did give us the freedom (opportunity) to develop our own senses of humor. What makes you laugh out loud? Why? Why do we laugh hardest sometimes at the misfortunes of others? And more importantly, why do we laugh at television sit-coms at all? What makes it necessary to make jokes about life, death, sex, heritage, race, and even the church? Well, I can't tell you because I wouldn't want anyone to stop laughing.

Enjoy the gift of laughter and keep on using your sense of humor. Don't let it go to waste. Develop a fair and honest basis for your laughter and laugh every day. Start out by just smiling at God's wonders. Remember, do unto others, and the whole world will laugh with you.

Somewhere in the universe, there is a great probability of a planet on which Adam and Eve obeyed God and did not eat of the forbidden fruit.

BAR HUMOR

Noah walks into a bar. The barkeeper asks, "What'll you have?"
Noah Responds, "Anything without water!"
Barkeeper: "Do you want some fruit juice?"
Noah: "That sounds good, and please put one of those little umbrellas in it."
Barkeeper: "Do you want something to eat with that?"
Looking at the menu, Noah answers, "Yes, I'll have the olive leaf salad, no dressing."

Moses walks into a bar. The barkeeper asks, "What'll you have?"
Moses: "Just some spring water, please."
Barkeeper: "Do you want something to eat with that?"
Moses: "Yes, I'll have the manna sandwich with snake meat, and make sure there aren't any locusts on it this time. And make sure the manna is fresh, none of that day-old stuff."

Jesus walks into a bar. The barkeeper asks, "What'll you have?"
Jesus: "May I have a glass of water, please? And could you put it in a wine glass?"
Barkeeper: "Do you want something to eat with that?"
Jesus: "Yes, I'll have the loaves and fishes sandwich, with just one mustard seed."

Paul walks into a bar. The barkeeper asks, "What'll you have?"
Paul: "I'll have the Prison Buffet - all the bread and water I
can eat!"

Adam and Eve walk into a bar. The "serpent" bartender says,
"We have a special on appletinis today!"

David walks into a bar. The barkeeper asks, "What'll you have?"
David: "Oh, just sling me a shot of that wine, on the rocks."
Someone else in the bar shouts, "Hey David, how about a psalm!
Do the country song about sleepin' in the green pasture."

Jonah walks into a bar. The barkeeper asks, "What'll you have?"
I'll have some spring water, no salt around the rim," Jonah
answers, "and I'm going on a boat trip later today, give me the fish
and chips!"

BIBLICAL TRUTH

The Word of God is sacred and inspired, not scared and despaired.

The population of the world today is estimated by the US Census Bureau to be 7.092 billion. That's 7,092,000,000. The population of the entire world in the year 1 AD is estimated to have been 200 million (200,000,000). The population of the United States is over 300 million now, as a comparison.

A single word from the Hebrew language in the Old Testament times and a single word from the Greek Hebrew of the New Testament times have multiple meanings in today's languages. The ancient word from the Hebrew which is translated as "day" in the Old Testament Genesis, for example, probably meant a period of time (day, month, year, millennia, hour, etc.).

The original manuscripts for the Old Testament were written in Hebrew. About 250 BC, legend has it that 72 scholars worked on putting the OT together for the Greek speaking Jews. The probability is higher that this legend is true at least for the Torah, the first five books of the OT. It is most commonly accepted that Moses was the author of, or at least dictated, the Torah. The discovery of the Dead Sea Scrolls in 1947 confirmed several of the writings of the Torah as well as Psalms and Isaiah. The Dead Sea Scrolls were found in a cave near the Dead Sea. In 2006, 70 or so small lead codices were found in a remote cave in eastern Jordan. The estimated dating of the scrolls was approximately 2000 years, and along with the text, included a map of Jerusalem which included depictions of the walls of the city and a cross marking what is probably the tomb of Jesus. Older documents help with the translation and confirmation of the existing translations available today.

The Bible is generally accepted by historians as being the most complete assembly of ancient writings which depict an accurate picture of what occurred during the early times in the Mediterranean area of the world.

The books of law in the Old Testament gave very detailed regulations regarding religion, government, daily activities, crimes, and punishments in the days of Moses.

The original manuscripts for the New Testament were written originally in the Greek – Hebrew. (This was a Greek translation of the Hebrew text for the Jews who spoke only Greek.)

Two Roman Emperors reigned during the life of Jesus. Caesar Augustus, of the "A decree went out from…" fame, ruled the Roman Empire until 14 AD. Following him was Tiberius Claudius Caesar Augustus who ruled until 37 AD.

The legitimacy of Jesus as the Son of God has always been in question. Many non-Christian religions claim that Jesus was a great prophet, teacher, and speaker, but not necessarily the Son of God. (None of them, however, deny that He existed.) In almost all other religions, the leaders or God-chosen ones have studied the teachings of Jesus in-depth before starting their own spiritual teachings.

Let us approach the legitimacy of the Son of God in another way. Try to imagine that a normal human (not the Son) was the son of a carpenter, learned his father's trade, and studied the

Torah scrolls and met with the temple leaders throughout his youth and early manhood. Is there any way that this man could have spoken and done everything that was involved in a self-made ministry? Jesus presented a new way to realize and understand God's grace as a loving Father and the path to everlasting life through the Messiah. Jesus never misspoke or answered questions wrong. He gave parables to help people understand and spoke for hours to large crowds (without notes!). He performed miracles and healings, even aware of when someone touched His cloak. And finally, He stated over and over again that He knew that He was the Son of God. It would be impossible for Jesus to just "wing it" whenever He spoke or performed miracles.

Jesus also prophesied in His speaking. As Matthew relates, Jesus spoke of the sign of Jonah, who spent three days in the belly of a fish. Not to mention the fish, who would have three days of indigestion. The Savior would spend 3 days in the heart of the earth, prior to The Resurrection.

Parables

Remember that the word "parable" is possibly from either the Greek "pair of bulls" or "pair of bowls", we aren't sure which. It may also be that the translation more closely means "a placing beside". There are just over thirty parables in the gospels. Jesus used parables as a way to illustrate the stories He told because so many of the people He spoke to were not always able to understand the true messages of the stories. The list of those who did not always understand includes not only the crowds, but the disciples, the priests, the rich, the poor, you, and me. The continuing challenge of helping people to understand parables now falls into the hands of the modern clergy. They hope to relate to us by comparing or illustrating parables by using examples from everyday life as it is today. It is by no means an easy task.

The Prophesy of Isaiah includes the proclamation that the Savior would use parables to illustrate because of the "spiritual dullness of the people". (From Matthew 13:13-14.)

The God Theorem: For every scientific argument denying the existence of God, there is an equal (and sometimes) opposite scientific argument proving the existence of God.

Jonah Goes on a Cruise

I want to re-tell you a story.

Jonah is one of the shorter books of the Bible (Old Testament, four chapters), with a big message. The most important thing to realize is that the story begins with Jonah as a prophet for God, and a very good and loyal one at that. A short version of the story goes something like this. God informs him that he is to go to Nineveh, a really bad place. Nineveh is an unkempt city with a very sinful population. It's the last place a man of God would choose to preach in. So, Jonah does what many of us choose when God gives us an order: he hops on a boat heading the opposite way. A storm comes up, the crew calls to their pagan gods and ask Jonah to pray to his God. Jonah, realizing what exactly has happened, tells them that he has disobeyed God and that the storm is his fault. To calm the storm, Jonah tells the crew that they must throw him overboard. This seems an extreme measure to the crew, so instead they begin to pray to Jonah's God for relief from the storm. (There is nothing like a bad storm in life to force an instant born-again reaction from people. I wonder if it lasted for the crew of the ship.)

Jonah finally convinces them to toss him, and when this is done the seas immediately calm down. But poor Jonah gets swallowed by a large fish (or whale). For three days. Jonah was "living" in a fish belly. Yuck. What does Jonah do? He praises and thanks God for saving his life and for leading him back to how he should have responded in the first place. The entire prayer is included in the second chapter. The fish throws Jonah up onto the shore (literally) after the allotted time, undigested and with a clarification of what he has to do next.

But it isn't all about the whale. Jonah made a beeline for Nineveh.

Now Jonah has regained his loyalty to God and gains many conversions quickly in Nineveh! His warnings about how God may destroy the city are wisely accepted by the citizens who turn from the dark side to God.

Three days later, though, Jonah gets mad at God! Apparently, he forgot again who the boss was! (Some of this is becoming frighteningly familiar to me all of a sudden!) The Gentiles of Nineveh were receiving God's compassion; Jonah wanted God's goodness for Israel, his homeland. Jonah now would rather die than to keep converting the "enemy" of his own people!

"But the Lord replied; 'Have you any right to be angry?'" (Jonah 4:4)

Now the great stuff; up to now the story is only good! Jonah goes outside of Nineveh and into the hot sun. God provides a vine to give "shade for his head", and Jonah was happy. But the next morning God sent a worm to destroy the vine, prompting Jonah to again wish he was dead rather than alive!

"But God said to Jonah, 'Do you have a right to be angry about the vine?'

'I do,' he said, 'I am angry enough to die.'

But the Lord said, 'You have been concerned about the vine, though you did not tend it or make it grow. It sprang up overnight and died overnight. But Nineveh has more than a hundred and twenty thousand people who cannot tell their right hand from their left and many cattle as well. Should I not be concerned about that great city?'" (Jonah 4:9-11)

This last verse is the end of the Book of Jonah. Why does God care about stupid people, and stupid cattle, and a great (?) city?

Two things come to mind. First, God's message is for everyone, not just specific areas of the world or races or even intelligence; God is also concerned for all living things of the world (cattle). Second, even God's best prophets got mad at Him for their misunderstanding of the mission at hand. Each of us can try our best to live the Christian life as God intended, but we will all lose focus at one time or another. The result of a backwards step is in which way the next step will go. Refocus, re-praise, re-pray, re-thank, reread, redefine, redirect, or re-ask; but respond and react with a forward step once again, with God's direction.

PROVERBS FROM THE
BOOK – OR ARE THEY?

Proverbs are observations of human behavior and advice about the wisdom of living a good and ethical life. Many of the statements are rather short. The simple definition of a proverb is an action word that has lost its amateur status (as in a "professional verb").

The majority of proverbs do not reference God at all, but account for the wisdom (which is referred to as "she") necessary to be a good Christian, or for that matter, a good person. There are several writers of the proverbs, but the majority of the book is attributed to Solomon.

Many of the following statements are from the book of Proverbs. (Reminder: All Bible references used in this book are from the NIV translation.) However, some are from different parts of the Bible, and some are just quotes from famous or not so famous people (perhaps even a movie quote, just to keep it interesting). Please take note: each one of these is taken out of context; they may or may not make sense without the remainder of the content. Test your memory and make an attempt to decide which of the following are from Proverbs and which are not.

Just to make sure no one goes crazy, the page following the last statement has a numbered list of where the statements originated, and in the case of the Bible quotes, the chapter and verse.

1. Rich and poor have this in common: the Lord is the Maker of them all.
2. All hard work brings a profit, but mere talk leads only to poverty.
3. But a witless man can no more become wise than a donkey's colt can be born a man.
4. Early to bed and early to rise makes a man healthy, wealthy, and wise.
5. If you find honey, eat just enough – too much of it, and you will vomit.
6. A perverse man stirs up dissention, and a gossip separates close friends.
7. A kindhearted woman gains respect, but ruthless men gain only wealth.
8. There are six things the Lord hates, seven that are detestable to him.
9. An honest answer is like a kiss on the lips.
10. A word aptly spoken is like apples of gold in settings of silver.
11. Praise the Lord all you nations; extol him, all you peoples.
12. Many women do noble things, but you surpass them all.
13. As a dog returns to his vomit, so a fool repeats his folly.
14. A man's ways seem innocent to him, but motives are weighed by the Lord.
15. A cheerful heart is good medicine, but a crushed spirit dries up the bones.
16. Hatred stirs up dissention, but love covers over all wrongs.
17. My husband is not at home; he has gone on a long journey.
18. Houses and wealth are inherited from parents, but a prudent wife is from the Lord.
19. Do not judge, for you too will be judged.
20. May the force of God be with you!

PROVERBS FROM THE BOOK – OR ARE THEY? ANSWERS!

Don't look until you read the 2 previous pages!

Was it as easy as you thought it would be? Actually 15 out of the 20 items were from the Book of Proverbs!

A list of references follows:

1. Proverbs 22:2
2. Proverbs 14:23
3. Job 11:12
4. Ben Franklin
5. Proverbs 25:16
6. Proverbs 16:28
7. Proverbs 11:16
8. Proverbs 6:16
9. Proverbs 24:26
10. Proverbs 25:11
11. Psalms 117:1, which is the shortest Psalm in the Bible, only 2 verses long.
12. Proverbs 31:29
13. Proverbs 26:11
14. Proverbs 16:2
15. Proverbs 17:22

16. Proverbs 10:12
17. Proverbs 7:19
18. Proverbs 19:14
19. Matthew 7:1, spoken by Jesus.
20. Okay, I made this one up, kind of. It could be from a movie that hasn't been made yet, though – like I said, it could be a quote from a not so famous person!

CHRISTMAS AND EASTER

Birth and Resurrection, Two Days To Celebrate!

A Christmas update:

As the Christmas season approaches once more, the story of the birth of Christ comes to the forefront. We are again in the midst of the rushing and the wrapping, the preparing and the parties, the decorating and the visiting, and the giving and the getting. But as we reflect on Christmases from the past, the wonder and retelling of the story renews our faithfulness and trust in the Newborn King.

"In those days Caesar Augustus issued a decree that a census should be taken of the entire Roman world. He (Joseph) went there (Bethlehem) to register with Mary, who was pledged to be married to him and was expecting a child." (Luke 2:1, 5.) Of course the all-important question that still burns in our minds is "Was Jesus born before or after the census was taken?" Indeed, if the census was taken for tax purposes, were Mary and Joseph permitted to receive a tax break from the addition to their family, or were they required to pay a full tax without the deduction? And did the Roman IRS guy question the situation regarding the fact that Mary was Joseph's betrothed? Or had they heard any of the talk that Joseph might not even be the father?

43

At Christmas, Mary and Joseph were directed to the stable, because the inn was full. But the stable was also probably full, due to the guests at the inn. Imagine the donkeys, cattle, sheep, and whatever else the people would have ridden to get to Bethlehem or cash in to pay their taxes. Then, shepherds show up with their sheep, which they couldn't leave behind. And finally, the Magi showed up with camels, more animals for the unstable stable area. Remember, none of the Bible books even specify that there were only three kings in the Magi group, a discrepancy which some say could have been upwards of twelve, with all the assistants and such.

And then there is the star. Was it a cluster of planets or stars or both, a comet, an asteroid, or just another miracle of the event?

God's Son, the Messiah, was born in the squalor of an old, crowded, and messy stable.

Youth to Adulthood

Unfortunately, but intentionally, we are left in the dark as to the childhood of Jesus. When reading from the second chapter of Luke, verses 40 to 52, we hear that He was consecrated and that, at twelve years of age, He was found in the temple with the teachers, listening, asking questions, and amazing them with His understanding. Other than a general statement about Him growing in knowledge and stature in verse 52, we lose touch with Him until He is about thirty years old.

I wonder if Jesus played, learned carpentry from Joseph, helped Mom Mary in the kitchen, or had to keep His room clean. Or did Jesus just study and pray as a teen and young man?

Did you ever wonder why Jesus (and God) waited until He was thirty years old to begin His teaching ministry? I don't know; but He sure was prepared by then! Maybe because Jesus and God both knew that with a decent bit of age He would gain wisdom. And with the experience as a "regular" person, Jesus would be better able to understand the people that He would be calling and speaking to in the future.

He had all the right answers, stories, explanations, and speaking abilities. When He called "soon to be" disciples, both He and they knew who He was talking to. The original disciples did not abandon Him as some followers did when they found out what the entire job description of disciple involved. (See John 6: 60-71)

Easter

Easter is the most important day to celebrate for all Christians. One of the most common musical genres in today's music happened on Easter. This genre is, of course, rock and roll, which honors the event of the rock being rolled away from the tomb and the resurrection of Jesus.

Easter occurs at the end of Passion Week, which begins with His triumphant entry into Jerusalem where Jesus is welcomed by faithful supporters, then continues on Thursday with the Last Supper when Jesus meets with his twelve disciples.

Good Friday represents possibly the lowest point in human history with respect to God's Son and the realization that all people from that point on would never be able to accept Jesus as Savior and Redeemer. The fall of man became complete in man's destruction of the One who was sent to teach and bring them to the close relationship which God desires with us.

Easter morning; the luminescent sun is rising over the horizon, Roman guards are awakening from a deep sleep, and the displaced stone is to the side of the tomb opening. It is a glorious bright sunrise indeed.

The guards run away, the women approach; they find that the tomb is empty. They listen to an angel, and a "gardener" is questioned by Mary as to the whereabouts of her Lord's lifeless body.

He is alive!

Jesus had provided, and continues to provide the most incredible evidence of a powerful and great King. A King of Kings who has conquered death. He has risen from the darkness of death by the hand and will of His Father. He has Risen to exist in the Life Everlasting.

There are many who spoke then and many who speak now saying "Give us a sign!"
YOU GOT IT! HE IS ALIVE!

The prophesies of the Old Testament are verified and documented by the events and writings of the New Testament. The NT describes the appearance of the physical Jesus during the ensuing days after the resurrection. But His appearance was not limited to just a few; He appeared to hundreds of people. The evidence is strong and for Christians, indisputable!

The book of John gives an extreme boost of confidence for the believers of today. Jesus allows Thomas to touch Him in order that Thomas might be convinced that is indeed the same body of Jesus that was destroyed.

"Thomas said to Him, 'My Lord and my God!'
Then Jesus told Him, 'Because you have seen Me, you have believed; blessed are those who have not seen and yet have believed!'" (John 20: 27-29)

THE TRINITY

The Holy Spirit

God, the Holy Spirit is one of the most difficult concepts to understand for most people. Am I filled with the Holy Spirit? Shouldn't I be different (think, feel, act, appear)? It doesn't seem consistent in my life. Can't I get a license or take a quiz to make sure I've got it right? Isn't there some kind of guidebook or manual? (The answer to the last one is yes!)

The Holy Spirit is not a ghost or an apparition. It has appeared in the Bible as a dove or fire. When you recognize that you are led to correct decisions every day by refusing to argue with the correct answer, God's answer, you are getting really close. Your responses, either verbalizations or actions, reflect your understanding of God's plan for His people and your life. We need to refuse to argue with the correct option by overcome the desires of personal gain, the possibility of failure, or the "easy way out".

So it is with the Holy Spirit. A spiritual existence is not always a religious existence and it is not always deep and specific enough to be considered a Christian existence.

God the Son

God the Son, the person of Jesus, is God's connection to us by His assuming the human form in order to communicate his Word directly, in addition to directives to the prophets and the church leaders of the Old Testament. Jesus also was the implement for presenting a new direction and choice for those who would accept and be able to understand the Everlasting Life.

What would have been the path of mankind if it were not for the fall? I can't help but wonder if all mankind would have lived a life with more of the attitude of Jesus, had the incident in Eden not determined our fates. Maybe we would still be in Gardens of Eden, with food available to all of us, and hearing God walking in the garden. Maybe we would even be capable of a deeper understanding of God, with no worries, and be able to glean answers easily for our questions with direct instructions from God. It would be paradise on earth! (Sigh.)

Of course, God knew that this would not be the case for us. But as it turns out, the way to paradise is the way to Eternal Life!

Jesus lived without sin, but still was faced with learning and studying, growing up as a carpenter, adjusting to family matters, and making His life meaningful. He called disciples who could not understand, could not remember anything, or even stay awake!

Even by the time Jesus said that one of the twelve would betray Him, each one still wondered aloud, "Is it I?" They were not positive of their own loyalty and belief, even then. On top of this, Jesus had to constantly deal with critics, government harassment, and jealous priests of the temple.

Jesus dealt with sinners of every kind: the poor, the sick, the rich, the fishermen, tax collectors, etc. And He felt joy, sadness, loss, compassion, frustration, and pain.

When Thomas sees and touches Jesus after the Resurrection, he immediately says "My Lord and my God". He realizes at this point that Jesus is not just the Messiah, but is also God! God in a form never seen before, and will not be seen again, at least for a while. Always keep in mind that doubt does not always mean unfaithful. We must strive to walk by faith and not by sight, which sounds like a great "sound bite" for several great songs which have been written.

God the Father

God is the Father of us all: Creator, Protector, Liberator, and Care-taker. When we refer to any part of the trinity, or even the trinity as a whole, many times the word we end up using is God.

Many of the verses in the Bible use this interchangeable wording. For instance consider this: "… but I will rejoice in the Lord. I will be joyful in God my Savior." The quote comes from the book of Habakkuk 3:17, another one of the short books of the Old Testament. Habakkuk is also responsible for generating one of today's popular phrases (as are many phrases used in popular culture): In 2:3, in reference to the future revelation, "The revelation awaits an appointed time…*wait for it…*"

APOLOGETICS

No Longer a Need To Apologize

Apologetics – "I'm a Christian, and I apologize. I'm really sorry."

This is not what the word apologetics means, and I am sorry that I misinterpreted it. However, I would like to apologize to all the non-believers who may be offended by my writing or speaking, and I apologize to God for the times I have not offended the non-believers when I should have. Someday, I hope to become a professional apologistician (not a word, but sounds good).

Apologetics is the discipline used in defending a position, such as: because of the nature of our country as it is today and what the founding fathers documents wrote, the Constitution should be changed to read "… Life, liberty, and the pursuit of unhappiness".

In Christianity, apologetics means to represent the defense and establishment of the Christian faith.

The defenses of the Christian faith usually fall into one of three main apologetic categories:

1. The validity of the Bible as fact and truth.
2. The resurrection of Jesus from the dead.
3. The origins of the earth, the universe, and the creation of life and the human race.

At times, a Christian is said to be a legalist, or that the Christian faith is too legalistic. I suppose they mean that we have too many rules, but actually, to be a legalist means having an improper fixation on law or codes of conduct for a person or group. Most of us would agree that Christianity does indeed focus on codes of conduct for both individuals and the Christian Family. And, there are certainly Commandments which need to be obeyed. However, the fixations or Commandments are anything but "improper". In fact, if anyone refers to us as legalists, we should point out that Christian citizens are subject to the system of laws enacted by the government just as all citizens of our country. Just because most of these laws are based on Biblical principles with regard to fairness for all, does not make Christians or Christianity "improper".

The greatest enemy to apologetics is the misuse, abuse, or misinterpretation of the Bible; or the misunderstanding of what God can do for you, and what you must do for yourself. We should do our best to avoid the set-backs of a do-it-yourself religion, a feed-my-ego religion (referring to the members or the leaders), or a feelings-only religion (don't think, only get emotionally involved).

God has given Grace to all, but we must be diligent in our studies and reading of the Word, we must work with, attend, and support our church, and we must be prepared to defend ourselves by speaking to non-believers without anger, but with firmness and confidence.

We are protected by God and nothing can come between us. Jesus keeps us from falling.

The Government of the People

The founding fathers did indeed specify a separation of church and state, but not actually an elimination of church from state. This was for the protection of the religious beliefs of the people coming from other places around the world.

The laws of our country support freedom of religion but not freedom *from* religion. At no time did the founding fathers eliminate God from their foundation for the government. In fact, they were extremely concerned about the effect of religion on government, but none of the laws created were promoting specific beliefs, but indeed followed the general concept of the Bible in how people should be treated and governed. Every individual citizen may share their religion with others, but the Constitution prohibits any "national" religion from operating the government.

The purpose of a national government is to defend the citizens of the nation or country from evil in the form of acts or deeds against them, ensuring the citizen's rights as equally as possible, and to protect and prosecute evil with appropriate retribution when absolutely necessary.

The purpose of Christianity is to reach the citizens in our own and all other countries. We are to teach the wondrous love of God through the teachings of Jesus, pray for the world, and extend the Word to those who are in other countries, including those who are evil to their citizens or against freedom and democracy as declared by God.

Incidentally, religion is taught in most of the countries of the world. The teaching is usually specific to a denomination or religion, but can also be a curriculum assigned to the concepts of religion in general. A country uneducated publically in religious teaching eventually becomes an un-churched country. Education is more of an "agenda" in the US as opposed to educating citizens as well rounded, knowledgeable human beings.

Christians = get the word to the unsaved.

Government = assess and administer justice.

As a citizen responding to the government, there are a myriad of problems that need to be worked out. Dissention and dissatisfaction have been caused by the lack of a basis of belief in the recent making of laws and decisions with regard to "the people as a whole". Without religion (plan, prayer, and commitment), laws will be enacted based on trends, and not an ethical or even a popular reason. These laws affect what will happen to society. There will no longer be laws which honor the majority vote; a few dozen people (activists) may be able to make decisions for an entire community in which they do not even live!

Now for the Christian response! I happen to live in a country where I don't practice my religion, I live my religion! My freedom has nothing to do with blowing up other people who don't believe as I do or even confronting them in the streets. I do object to them attacking God and Christianity. I must consider my religion in determining my opinions just as other religious groups do (or should do).

Besides, my short time here is insignificant to the eternity I will spend when I graduate to heaven!

In God we trust. What a strong statement! It's stamped and printed on our money, but not on our credit cards. (That bothers me, does it bother you?) As we think this through though, it occurs to me that the government of the US legislated that this "motto" be put on all of our money. I trust God more than the government. It may be the most democratically structured government in the world, but it has been compromising the laws it has passed as the years have gone by since the money motto was first enacted. The reliability and strength in God is in the back of their minds, replaced by the supposed "will of the people" and the power of the vote.

God is probably not getting much satisfaction in knowing that Christian church education and churches are available almost everywhere in the US, but that in public schools religious education, even in general terms of reference, is totally illegal. Religion is not being taught because the few are against it, and the many are overcome with apathy, egotism, and greed. Of course, I don't care, because I'm the most important, and I want to make sure I get better than my share! Wow, I hope that the previous statement was just a burst of sarcasm, I would hate for that to be true!

The Non-believers

I love non-Christians and non-believers. I can and do get along with the best of them. We must all remember that our main purpose toward those persons is to pray that they may somehow, someday find their way to the acceptance of Jesus as their Lord and Risen Redeemer, and they come to a personal and understanding relationship with God. We create hope for all when we continue to pray for them, and they can't make us stop. If they ever ask me to stop praying for them, I always answer, "Sorry, I'm not permitted to stop".

Use caution when speaking to non-believers. Remember they are already offended that the subject has come up, and all of their defense shields will be up and their arguments will come to the forefront. They have what they consider to be both logical and emotionally sound beliefs in mind, just as you should. Nothing is to be gained by shouting or fighting over differences. Once emotions come out, we end up merely exchanging opinions which are shallow as opposed to the Truth which need to be brought forward.

Don't knock it!

Jesus answers the door and also knocks on it. In Matthew, Jesus describes the "ask, seek, knock" scenario. "Ask and it will be given, seek and find, knock and the door will be opened to you." He continues with "for everyone who asks will receive, seeks will find, and to him who knocks, the door will be opened." (Matthew 7: 7-8, paraphrased)

Then, later, Jesus states: "Here I am! I stand at the door and knock. If anyone opens the door, I will come in and eat with him, and he with Me." As I said this comment was made later, much later. Just to remind you, this particular statement is in Revelation 3:20! It is listed among one of the seven scrolls sent to the seven churches by John as was commanded by his revelation. Each Revelation scroll was dictated to each individual church by the "Living One; I was dead, and behold I am alive forever and ever!" (Revelation 3:18) Each one of the scrolls was specific as to "what is now, and what will take place later." (3:19)

We have to continuously develop our own relationship with Christ and God. He may be constantly knocking, but if we don't knock back, the two way relationship never goes anywhere.

FAVORITE BIBLE STORIES

The following are excerpts from some of my favorite Bible stories. A lot of times I do not remember the correct quotes or even the exact story itself. You may have to look them up if you don't think these are exactly correct!

The First Last Supper

After Jesus told the disciples in the upper room that one of them would betray Him, one of the disciples asked, "Is it me?'

Jesus corrected the disciple, "I."

Disciple: "Did you say aye, as in yes?"

Peter: "No, He said I as in me."

Disciple: "You're going to betray Him?

Peter: "No, not me; I mean I! Can't you understand English?"

Spreading The Word

Peter was the rock upon which Jesus said that He would build His church. He was one of the closest disciples of Jesus. Mary Magdalene was the first female version of an early disciple, and believed that Jesus was who He said He was. (The following is not in the Bible.) At one point after the resurrection, Peter and Mary set out as a team to preach and teach the people about Jesus. When Paul first came to Jerusalem to preach, he met up with them and they decided to combine their efforts and present their story to a large crowd. It was at this meeting when they broke into song, that they became collectively known as Peter, Paul, and Mary.

Doubting Thomas

This refers to the disciple Thomas, who is rarely mentioned in the gospels. After the Resurrection of Jesus, the other disciples told Thomas about seeing Jesus. But Thomas wouldn't believe them unless he himself could see the nail prints in the hands of Jesus, and touch the wound in His side. Then Jesus appeared to the roomful of people and said something about Thomas being a lousy disciple for not believing after He had told them that He would be resurrected. And the rest of the disciples just told Thomas, "We told you so!"

The Inn

When Jesus was about to be born, Joseph and Mary were looking for a place to stay, because everything was full and they didn't make online reservations. An innkeeper was kind enough to let them sleep in his garage. The rest is history, except for the little known fact that because of this special night, a hotel chain known as the Holiday Inn Stable was developed in order that people would have a place to stay when travelling on the holidays. The flaw in the original plan was that the inn would only be open six days a year, on holidays, and they ended up staying open other days too.

The Loaves and the Fishes

This event happened when Jesus was speaking to a very large crowd, and they were hungry and the concession stands were all closed. So Jesus asked the disciples what was available and they found that there was one basket with loaves and fishes in it. Jesus blessed the food, and when it was passed around there were multigrain breads and sushi for everyone, with some left over for a snack later.

The Parable of the Weed

A farmer planted wheat seed in his fields, but at night his enemy came into his fields and planted weed among the wheat. When the farmer's workers saw the weed, they asked the farmer, "Should we pull the weed?"

The farmer responded, "No! Pulling the weed will loosen the soil around the wheat, and it will not grow properly. Wait until the wheat is ready to harvest, then pull the weed first, bundle it, and then burn it. Then we can harvest the wheat."

This was a great plan by the farmer, except that the smoke from burning the weed made the workers incapable of harvesting the wheat for several days and nights. I believe the meaning of this parable is that they should not burn weed until the work is done.

(The actual parable, as well as the explanation, is in Matthew 13:36-43.)

FAVORITE BIBLE VERSES

Sometimes I don't remember all of the words correctly, so you may have to look them up to check the actual wording. I have included the references for you to check!

It was her fault. (Genesis 3:12 –"The woman you put here with me - she gave me some fruit from the tree, and I ate it.")

With God all things are possible, but He gets to choose what things, not us. (Matthew 19:26, Mark 10:27)

In the beginning, God made it happen. (Genesis 1:1)

I boast gladly about my weaknesses, but watch out for my strengths. (2nd Corinthians 12:9)

A time to weep, a time to laugh, a time to laugh harder. (Ecclesiastes 3:4)

How many times must I forgive my brother? Not seven, but seventy-seven times. So seventy-eight is the magic number! (Matthew 18: 21-22)

Let the little children come unto Me ... heaven belongs to such as these; except for Little Bully Billy over there. (Matthew 19:14-15)

The Greatest Commandment- "Love the Lord your God with all your heart and with all your soul and with all your mind...Love your neighbor as yourself."

The Pharisees respond, "aha, that's two not one!" (Matthew 22: 37-40)

Jesus is strong and I am weak, but I work out. (2nd Corinthians 12:10b)

And God saw that laughter was very good. (I'm sure I remember that from somewhere in Genesis.)

The Lord is my sheep bird, I shall not haunt. (Psalm 23:1)

Sarah said, "God has brought me laughter, and everyone who hears about this will laugh with me." Sarah had just given birth to Isaac. She was 90 years old and Abraham was 100. Better brush up on the parenting skills! (Genesis 21:6)

Don't you know your body is a temple? —Mine is a temple of doom! (1 Corinthians 6:19)

PRAYER - SIN, FORGIVENESS, AND ATONEMENT

Prayer

Prayer is one of the easiest things to carry out in the daily Christian life; we just bow our heads and speak to God, either aloud or in silence. One of the hardest things to do correctly in living the Christ-life is to pray comfortably and effectively. The instructions are easy enough, when we are told "to pray in this manner", and then recite the Lord's Prayer, which He taught to his disciples. However, note that the Lord's Prayer is not to be only recited, but also to be used as a basis for all of our personal prayers.

When you do pray, pray with praise, whether it is good news or bad. God gave up his Son, who brought us all the teachings we need to carry out God's plan for us, before dying for our sins. All situations for Christians are sanctioned by the all-knowing God, and He assists us in the path to everlasting life. In this way, you continually acknowledge God's presence in your life and don't call on Him only when you need Him or have a problem. Pray persistently for those things which are meant to serve God and further His kingdom on earth, because that is our main purpose. And pray for all things (Ephesians 6:18); bring everything to the table.

Listen for an answer to your prayers and be ready to act upon God's answer. Don't always shrug something off as a "bad idea". Be sure our answer is not "It's too much (or time consuming, or too hard, or too risky)!" Or, "I'm not ready (or not smart enough, or I'm too smart, or I can think of an easier way)!" Remember Isaiah's response, "Send me!"

Lord, how should we pray?

We start by addressing God as our hallowed Father, residing in Heaven and acknowledge that His Kingdom will come and that His will shall come to pass here on the earth the same way it does in Heaven. We ask Him for things which we need, but only on a daily basis. He will provide for us today, but we must return to prayer tomorrow to continue the process of each day's provisions. Bread is not food or money, but the sustenance that will keep us in faith and strength for this day.

We all are trespassers, debtors, or transgressors. No matter which word is used, in all cases it can be interpreted to mean "sinners". However, note that we must truly (in mind, heart, word, and deed) forgive others before we are to be forgiven by God for our own sins.

Ask and we shall receive deliverance from "the evil one". We also ask God for protection from the temptations of evil. We all face specific temptations every day, sometimes repeatedly, and sometimes not even recognizable as evil in nature. (If it is too good to be true, it probably isn't true! – as one example.)

Love your enemies, pray for them; but when it is necessary, protect yourself from the evil one(s). Remember to analyze temptations from a Christian perspective using Jesus' teachings, prayer, the effect on others, and the consequences of the actions you take.

We again should end our praying with reaffirming God's power and glory. God wants us to have the power He alone can supply. Often we know about the power, but are not using it. If we are able to keep God first in our lives, then not only will we receive His support, but we become the people God is looking for when He needs earthly assistance from someone with our particular gifts. Don't miss opportunities!

Repent of your sins! Join SS now! (Sinaholics Synonymous)

Repentance demands the attempt to overcome the sin which has been committed, atonement demands that recompense be made by the sinner to God and anyone sinned against, and the forgiveness is free! Always free!

The accusers of Jesus always had problems with finding an actual law that He was breaking. They often attempted to entrap Him with pointed questions, resulting in either a profound refuting of the topic itself, a parable illustrating the ambiguity of the topic, or an equally disturbing question thrown back to the accusers.

And they asked Jesus, "Are you a good Jew, or a bad Jew?"

When you want to be guided in your prayer, and are interested in how Jesus prayed, read Chapter 17 in the Book of John. In it, Jesus prays for himself (verses 1-5), then for his disciples (verses 6-19), and then for all believers, including us (verses 20-26).

Why do bad things happen to good people? Because that is the way of life! True Faith is not calling on God when only bad things occur, but calling on God daily and accepting ALL things which occur and confirming your continued Faith and commitment to Him.

The suffering of humankind was brought about by the deal in Eden. Adam and Eve were created by God but now lived with the freedom of choice along with His guidance and care. Because of the Satan snake, the freedom was doomed and became the choice of accepting the offerings of God as opposed to just getting them. We were left to endure pain and suffering with or without God. But the choice of freedom through faith would always be available for the asking.

With pain and suffering came the most dreadful of life events, starting with Adam and Eve. They lost a child to an early death. Plus, the murderer was also their child, the eldest, who would be ejected from the family because of his selfish actions. The first two children born to Adam and Eve were "lost" due to the work of the evil one which had been let loose by their own sin. The "first family" was not off to a good start.

A Path for Problems

Is the current issue you are having just a problem, is it a PROBLEM, or is it a CRISIS? A CRISIS is an issue which has life-changing or eternal life implications. Most other issues are PROBLEMS or problems which will make no difference in the long run.

The path to following Jesus is spelled out in the gospels with additions in the later books of the New Testament by the apostles, Paul, and others. As it ends up, the reading of the Bible is the easy part of the process. To follow in the correct path which God has set for you involves individual consideration and prayer, as well as additional information, service, and the use of your talents in service to Him. Application of your understanding is the key. This use of God's plan through Jesus is more up to you than to God. You must accept the challenge set forth by the Savior, a challenge which is ever-present to you from God in forms which you must learn to recognize.

What about the "last-ditch" effort? Why not use the death-bed confession approach and get on with a self-centered, get ahead at all costs, sinful life until the last minute? How about an unpardonable sin? (There is no such thing when you think about it.) All sins can be forgiven, but an insincere, untrue death-bed confession cannot fool God. If you know of the severity of your sins, then the confession lacks the love, honesty, conviction, understanding, and conversion that one is aware of already. I wouldn't want to bet on being able to pull it off at the last second.

The healing power of the human body as commissioned by God is truly amazing. The body has many automatic systems to take care of it as well as warning signs when something is wrong, as long as they are not ignored. Even after major surgery, healing takes place by the body with assistance from the advancement of diagnosis, research, specialized knowledge, improved medications, and modern equipment.

In Second Corinthians, Paul tells us to "be of good courage". Courage is a valuable asset, but it is not always "good" courage. Paul's intention of good courage involves the knowledge and ability of Christians to be able to deal with the problems of this earth by keeping in mind the ultimate goal of our lives: to end up with more money and possessions than the rest of the human race. No, sorry, that's not right! It also is not the guy with the most toys wins! The ultimate goal of our lives should be: to praise and serve God because of the sacrifice of Jesus, so that we may attain a final afterlife in heaven. Are my goals pleasing and dedicated to God, or myself? Ambitious goals should be focusing on God to ensure our success in heaven.

Worried? Think of how Jesus spoke in Matthew 6:25 and 27. "Therefore I tell you, do not worry about your life, what you will eat or drink; or about your body, what you will wear. Is not life more important than food, and the body more important than clothes? Who of you can add a single hour to his life?"

"Stairway to heaven" is a phrase used to describe our journey through our earthly life. Each step on the staircase is on the pathway to our reward in the heavenly mansion. The rewards we are investing in to receive in eternal life are far greater than anything we could imagine with these earthly minds and bodies. Invest in your after future!

"Go and sin no more." If it were only that easy.

We all sin, sin is sin, and there is no true ranking of severity for sin.

Biblically, divorce is only permitted if a spouse is unfaithful.

"Thou shalt not kill" has become "Do not murder." (NIV)

If there are no lines to be drawn, then do not draw any lines.

The judge and the jury are not here. No one on earth can determine who will and who will not make it to heaven.

FASTING FOR A LIFETIME

I fast on a limited basis for short times, or limit certain foods at different times. I call this slow fasting. Recently though I have reconsidered and may eventually try fast fasting.

Fasting is the process of going without food for a specific amount of time in order to atone (make up for) sins committed, or, as in the case nowadays, to lose as much weight as possible within the next twenty-four hours for a doctor's appointment or a weigh-in at the gym. In Biblical times, fasting was usually associated with atonement or a specific reason within the doctrine of certain religious sects.

Fast fasting can feature fast foods, French fries, fruit flies, first flaming fondues, fruit pies, flipped flapjacks, filleted flounder, fattening fudge, flamed franks, fried fish, frosty floats, and fabulous fresh frozen fizza, um, pizza.

Further fast fasting fads occur from February for forty days, otherwise known as Lent. Forty day fasting helps us to fit into frocks for Easter, for it falls at the close of Lent. (I once gave up lint for Lent, but that lends to a later literary listing.)

He who fasts first shall be last, but he who fasts last shall be the first last faster.

BAD NEWS, GOOD NEWS, GREAT NEWS

I've got bad news and I've got good news; and then I've got the greatest news of all!

The bad news:

All of us are sinners. Evil will always exist in the world and some evil will tempt us, no matter where we are in our walk in the faith.

None of us knows when or if we will be worthy of heaven.

Natural disasters, war, persecution, suffering, poverty, tragedy, and death are present with us.

Illness, disease, unhappiness, pride, mistrust, doubts, questions, being rich or poor, stress, and disappointment - are all part of the earthly life.

The Good News:

We have the Good News in the written form. We have instructions and help.

We are worthy of accepting God's will and plan for our lives.

Christians have a great chance of Eternal Life, an inactive Christian has a good chance, non-believers have a slim chance, and atheists haven't got a prayer.

We know God through His direct contact from His Son, His servants, His apostles given to us as teachings, history, and illustrations in the Bible.

We are forgiven and we can forgive. We have help, providing we seek and receive the assistance in the proper manner, mindset, and heart set.

The GREATEST NEWS of all:

The power of the combined resources of Christians redeemed by Jesus and protected by God is infinite.

We may become worthy by our obedience, prayer, and service with the trust and support of Our Savior and Our God.

We can become capable of passing the word of God to others by using the Truth in our message and the Power of God as our basis.

We are not alone on earth or in heaven. The bad news mentioned above is illuminated or eliminated by dedicated, commissioned, and compassionate Christians who serve God and all people of the world, not for who they are, but because they need help.

EVERLASTING LIFE

When you think of God, keep two words first and foremost: omnipotent and infinite. God is omnipotent, as in all-powerful and all-knowing; God is infinite, as in always, never-ending and never-beginning.

When you think of Life, keep two words first and foremost: service and everlasting. Life is service to God and His children; Life is everlasting through faith and forgiveness as promised by God.

When you think of God and Life, keep the basic needs first and foremost which lead to Everlasting Life: love, prayer, praise to God, service to God's Church, service to others, study of The Bible, thankfulness, sin and the forgiveness of sin.

When you think of Everlasting Life, keep in your heart the promise of God for us through His Son and our Savior Jesus Christ.

If we don't achieve a personal relationship with God, then climate change is just God's way of saying – you'd better get used to the heat!

Disciple, Apostle, Saint, Prophet

A Disciple is a follower, a student, and a pupil. An Apostle is a representative, a delegate, or perhaps an ambassador of someone else that is sent out to educate others. So basically the disciple is a learner and an apostle is one who lives and preaches what he has learned. A Saint is a great Apostle who remembers that he always will be a disciple. In other words, the men who were called by Jesus were disciples, but eventually were promoted to being apostles. A Prophet is a disciple who is given insight by God into what will come to be Truth in a future scenario.

Not all disciples are apostles, but all apostles are disciples.

Brainwork

Scientists estimate that we use only 10% of the ability of our brains. (I am striving for 10%, but have only reached 9.45 %.) We cannot imagine what insights and knowledge we could learn, or even retain, with a few more points of brain ability. Remember in school, a 10% is a pretty low score. Sometimes putting your first and last name on the paper would not even get you 10%! Without learning, imagination, and God, we will never pass the grading scale that our life requires. Using 100% of the brain's ability still does not help us reach God's infinite knowledge and capabilities, but it would be exciting to be able to think more deeply and comprehend more about our reasons for earthly existence, the concepts of the different types of love, and how we could be more understanding of each other, etc, etc.

Different uses of the same words in phrases can mean vastly different things. There are heart phrases: heartache, heartburn, heartbeat, heart attack, affair of the heart, heart surgery, and love God with all your heart. And using a different word, there are dead phrases: dead tired, dead weight, dead-head, dead man's float, dead man walking, walking dead, dead to the world, dead-end job, He has risen from the dead.

The meanings of words and phrases are constantly being distorted and misunderstood by nearly everyone, including ourselves, by not listening and speaking carefully. There is a great amount of difference between a broken heart and a heart attack.

Note that the heart phrases don't always have something to do with the heart and the dead phrases are not always about the death of the body. Several phrases from each group are physical and some are mental.

At a very young age, I learned a hard lesson by re-phrasing an age-old compliment. In trying to impress a young lady that I had a fondness for, instead of telling her that "she made time stand still", I upgraded it and told her that "she had a face that could stop a clock".

Water and Fire

Water (floods, rain, hurricanes) and fire (forest fires, house fires) can be man-made or "natural" disasters. Water and fire (heat in some form) are as much a necessity of life as food and shelter. But uncontrolled, they can become dangerous and destructive.

The Bible uses water and fire many times for analogies to other facets of our lives. Fire becomes both the symbol of an anointing of the Holy Spirit upon the apostles as well as a useful descriptor of hell. Water floods the earth and kills a pharaoh and his soldiers as well as becomes the Living Water for all to drink and the conveyance rite of baptism. The living water is a manageable flood.

When you think of Jesus Christ, keep the following in mind: God, Life, Everlasting Life.

GRANDPA

I'm still trying to adapt and understand the full concept of being a Grandpa.

There are brand new people in my life that need the love and care that are reserved for close family members. Are there really new human beings that I can love as much as my own children? Yes, there are.

I am re-learning that time does slow down. These young people live for the day, no, for the moment. There are new words for me to learn, things that I need to re-learn how to re-teach.

But most of all, I get to take time to play again. I don't mean the playing of games or the playing of everyday adulthood, but playing. You know toys and imagination and forgetting about the time. I'm talking about playing with pots and pans, cars and trucks, stuffed animals and repetitive contraptions, dolls and tea sets, blankets and pillows, cardboard boxes and paper. And I'm reading to someone who listens and enjoys every word and picture. And coloring, oh the coloring!

Speaking of imagination, I am also entranced by things which I have observed that are new to the grandchildren. Exploring the inside of a new area of a house- a room, pictures, furniture, tall people, child-size people, a spot on the rug, available food, pets, sitting, crawling, climbing. Exploring the outside of anywhere- trees, grass, houses, flowers, stones, birds and bugs.

Even though many of us were parents of our own children, by the time we become grandparents, we have forgotten how quickly the child-like mind absorbs and progresses. During dinner the other night, my grandson had gobbled up several carrot sticks which I had just put on his plate. Two weeks ago, when I asked him where his food went, he said, "It went in my mouth, and down, down, down into my tummy!" This time, only two weeks later, I asked where the carrot sticks went that I had put there a minute ago. He pointed to his mouth and said absolutely nothing at all. Even though no one else was listening, I felt like an idiot. He looked at me as though I should have a very good idea what happened since he had explained it to me just recently.

Again I am reminded that keeping a child-like mind as an adult has definite advantages. I know I am supposed to be grown up and all, but my mind absorbs and progresses more quickly when things are clear and not muddied and muddled by unimportant issues and problems of everyday drudgery.

NAPPING

Did you ever hear the results of a scientific study that you could disprove immediately if the scientists would just ask YOU? I have had this very reaction to studies on napping. The length of the nap depends on what each individual finds what their ideal nap time is.

It's like dieting. There are still basic rules that need to be followed. And it is like the Christian Life (or the Christ-like life) which also has basic rules which need to be followed.

Let us discuss napping. Napping is the activity of sleeping during the day or when it is not the traditional time to sleep (usually considered to be at night). Recently, I read and heard that studies show that naps should be no more than 30 minutes long to be "most effective" for your health and well being. However, in the past, we have also heard and read about the benefits of short power naps, long and longer naps, and no naps (because there is no way to catch up on sleep). At one point, the rule was sleep either shorter than twenty minutes or longer than an hour. Every once in a while, the topic of nap length comes up in conversation, and opinions seem to vary immensely. A lot of scientific research and investigation has provided so much exhaustive information that the scientists have had to take naps after doing the research. The truth seems to be that it all depends upon what your personal experience and findings have been. We all amass our own intelligence gathering and nap for how ever long is needed and/or agreeable for our own situations.

Napping is slightly akin to our Christian Life. The amount of time we invest in preparing and executing God's plan using the example of Jesus in our own lives can vary as much as the lengths of the disputed nap times.

Don't nap when you should be doing. Do nap when you need to. However, be careful not to nap like the disciples did in Gethsemane. They got into big trouble with Jesus. They couldn't stay awake for even one hour; this still happens sometimes in church services every week around the world (for various reasons).

By the way, I am not napping or resting my eyes; I am either praying or creating more thoughtful ideas to write about, with Divine Inspiration, of course. And that is not snoring; it's just speaking in tongues.

FEAR OF GOD

Thank You for the world so sweet,
Thank You for the food we eat,
Thank You for the birds that sing,
Thank You God for everything.

Sometimes, when I am going into a meeting or a stressful situation and don't have time to pray, I just think about the last line of this children's prayer. It has become a key phrase that gives me immediate calmness and clarity and puts a smile on my face. It's almost too simple (minded) to admit.

"It will put the fear of God into you!"
This is an old phrase that is hardly used at all anymore, mainly because no one is afraid of God in these times. No one fears a loving God.

However, those who should fear God are those who are without Him. We are given every opportunity to come into His arms, even though many still shy away. Without God there is no comfort, guidance, true love, direction, trust, and on and on. With God, earthly life is more joyful, and the prospect for the future is even better: Everlasting Life.

There is another "fear of God". Yes, God is omnipotent and fears nothing, but He does have one frustrating "fear". Since the fall of mankind in the Eden garden, He has been constantly calling

His children to resist evil, temptation, and to live by His Word. He even sent His Son, Jesus, to help get us back on track by dying for our sins. Jesus left us a tremendous catalog of teachings to live by, all wrapped up in a Bible which is available as a guide not only for everyday life, but a guide to life after death.

We need to answer His call with prayer, read His Word, and promote His kingdom with attendance in church, financial support, the development of Christian relationships, and direct service to Him using the talents which He has provided for each of us. We ought to be asking for assistance to seek out our own individual talents and use them to the greatest of our ability to further His glory while we are here on earth.

God appreciates us, and welcomes our praise, prayers, and service.

The army with God as their counselor will protect those who cannot protect themselves. Any government or military which imprisons and destroys the lives of its own citizens is destined to be brought to earthly justice through governmental sanctions and judgment by the rest of the world.

And, for heaven's sake, seek help from our Christian leaders, church family, and other Christians when assistance or support is needed. What you seek from God is not always what you get, and God's answer is sometimes no, but always keep in mind that "With God all things are possible".

Work

Over the years, I have been interested in work satisfaction. The career changes I have personally made over the years have not always been positive as far as advancement or money is concerned. The fact is, I have always felt, and now know, that I can do many jobs well and can be satisfied and happy doing different things. But I have always known in the back of my mind who was the real boss, even though I know that sometimes I "didn't have the time" to consult God on many daily decisions. In other words, God wasn't in my thoughts every minute of the day.

I have found that "every minute of the day" is the wrong phrase to use. Having a major thought process of God in the forefront of my mind makes each minute of the day easier to face. With the prospect of Everlasting Life, earthly life is just a prelude to the really good stuff. Work is play, interactions are meaningful, problems are minor, success is triumphant, and anything that happens with God's Christians is pure joy.

The Powerlessness of Positive Stinking

The concept of positive thinking can be a source of great power. However, in misuse, it can also be a powerless factor in our lives. And that stinks.

Positive thinking has long been the mantra of many successful people when discussing how and why they are successful. The topic of positive thinking has also been a factor in many writings and speeches which are aimed at making others in the world successful. If you toss in the additional secrets and attractions "theories" which are used to make us successful, the information on self-help is so abundant that we have all become successful and happy. If you are not, maybe it's your own fault and you should go out and buy some books, listen to some speeches, watch some videos, or all of the above.

Please don't let positive thinking become positive stinking. Perhaps the better term to use is Positive Christian Living. Positive Christian Living is not based on self, but on what we should say or do according to God's Way and the effect upon others. Strive to walk in the path of Jesus, not the path of material success.

We need to think positively twice (God's way and the effect on others) before speaking or acting in a Positive Living manner.

God wants His churches and His people to have POWER! The Power of the Almighty is available and waiting to be used. To be able to possess and use this power requires the prerequisites of understanding what the power is and how it is to be used. Forget personal or church gain or fame, forget an easy way out or a free pass in, and forget going your own way and not remembering Who is in charge. POWER! Use it or lose it!

DO UNTO OTHERS THE JESUS WAY

Do unto others … I goofed up …again …still.

We have grown up in a society where one of the most common and quoted statements by Jesus is used in ways that Jesus did not mean. "Do unto others as you would have them do unto you." (Matthew 7:12 or Luke 6:31)

My upbringing included getting along with all people and respecting their rights, lives, and opinions. This is wrong if I remain silent and do not defend my own equally legitimate rights, life, and opinions. My life should be respected also. And so it shall be.

Going to church is necessary to worship, praise, pray, and learn with God and His people (and our church family) in His house. Serving in the church with our specific talents and tithes are a part of our worship and praise for that which God has given us.

But as Christ has shown us, our actual service, life-work, prayer, and study are not in the church building, but in our home, work place, and social activities. These are the places where the real duties of a Christian take place.

Persistence with Jesus as our example always should be our response, rather than resisting a conflict or upsetting someone else. We should not give in - demand the respect for what you believe in!

Speaking of your talents, they can be in many forms. Basically, your talents are what you are good at in a natural way, that you can be yourself, and serve God and the rest of civilization. This alone is almost impossible to do when others expect something else from you.

The arts, both the participation in, and the appreciation of, are extensions of ourselves in particular directions. Some Christians use their talents in the arts to glorify God and Jesus, and should be supported in their efforts. The artists themselves must be ever mindful of where their gifts come from and how they are to apply themselves totally to the mission at hand; making themselves and those who appreciate them more loving and understanding Christians.

In living the Christian Life, remember how much God has provided for us. One of our goals should be to serve with as much love as we are receiving. In other words, keep your focus on what God wants and what Jesus gave to us. The gifts we have accepted without thanks or service are given without a price tag, but were not on sale, and did not have any rebates or coupons associated with them. Our quest, duty, obligation, return service, or whatever we need to call it is to respond automatically. We should react with praise, thankfulness, servitude, and use the gifts and talents we have to further enhance His Kingdom. It does no one any good to keep to ourselves what we have been freely given.

Impossible Mission

Is it impossible to make Christians of everyone in the world? In a word: yes.

Our mission on earth is to make disciples of Jesus Christ, each in our own way. There have always been and always will be doubters and unbelievers that have either been misled or have succumbed to the evil one. We are to help build a contingent of current and future Christians who are armed to understand that being a Jesus freak is what God wants, but not what the world may understand.

Included in this challenge is ministry to the poor, fighting hunger, and combating diseases in God's world.

Have you quit searching for God's purpose for you in this life? Don't stop looking, praying, listening, studying, and talking to others about your concerns. It is not worth wasting your life now and losing eternal life.

In Ephesians 6:10-18, Paul tells us about the armor of God, none of which can be used in actual hand-to-hand warring combat, but all are necessary for us to arm ourselves for the battle of Christianity. This armor includes: the belt of truth, the breastplate of righteousness, feet fitted with readiness from the Gospel, the shield of faith, the helmet of salvation, and the sword of the spirit! Each piece of armor has a purpose, not only to fight with our enemies and Satan, but to protect ourselves and our bodies from harm. The power behind this armor is unbeatable and indestructible when it comes to protecting the promise of our everlasting life.

In Ephesians 5:1, Paul tells us to be "imitators of God, therefore, as dearly loved children." We are children, and God is the Father of all, and can be trusted and loved back as our primary caretaker.

In another part of Ephesians (2:8-10), Paul instructs that "by grace you have been saved, through faith – and not from yourselves, it is the gift of God – not by works, so that none can boast. For we are God's workmanship, created in Christ Jesus to do good works, which God prepared in advance for us to do."

Interesting Observations On The Bible and Life in General

King David wrote many of the Psalms. He was the first winner in the rap category for both performing and composing.

Try to imagine if there were restaurants during Jesus' time. One restaurant in Jerusalem was popular for honoring the Roman leaders. An ancient menu has been found which lists some of the specials: The Roman Emperor Salad Special- a Caesar salad (seasonal, only available during Augustus); The Governors Special- an all-you-can-eat buffet nicknamed the "Plentious Pile-it"; and the Galilean Special- "Pickled Herod".

All of us are sinners. The Ten Commandments are the basic rules and regulations set down by God for us. All other laws should be made with regard to these laws. In our desire to make things more modern, there has been some adaptation to the originals to keep us more comfortable and make it easier to be good followers in our own religions. For instance, nowadays many Jewish people believe 7 out of The Ten Commandments need to be followed. Many Christians believe that probably 5 are enough.

Dyslexic Bible reader: In the beginning was doG.

Did you hear about the insomniac, dyslexic, and agnostic person? He stayed up all night wondering about the existence of doG.

"Can I have dessert?" I asked as a child.

"Finish the food on your plate first, there are people starving in many places." was the reply.

I never could figure out how my eating everything given to me would help starving people who were not anywhere near my home. It just didn't make any sense. So I wrapped up the food I wasn't going to eat and tried to mail my leftovers to the people overseas. I guess that wasn't exactly how it worked. The overseas people were not happy, my parents weren't happy, and I think the Post Office wanted me to eat the food when it eventually was returned.

I am writing a modern Children's Christmas story: "Fear not, for I bring you glad tidings of great toys!" This proclamation was announced to the sheep-nerds a-hiding in the fields.

When preparing presents at Christmas, I usually listen to wrap music.

I am in the process of cutting up a very large tree in my yard. I have cut off all the limbs and shaped the top into a fine point. Now, to complete it, I am going to cut a very large section of the trunk out at the bottom, to shape it into like a tunnel. Then, I will call the whole thing a needle and rent a camel to take through the eye of it.

I like the kind of theological discussion with my fellow Christians that are easy to defend, but not a complicated disagreement that gets everyone upset. One of my favorites was when I heard a friend say, "God can't lie."

I said, "Of course He can lie!"

My friend babbled, "I can't believe you said that! God can't lie to the people He loves. Why would you even think of that? Tell me one time He has lied."

"I didn't say that He did, I said that He can or could lie. God is still omnipotent. He can do anything He wants to do. If you would have said God doesn't lie, I would have totally agreed with you."

It's amazing. One little word and someone can take it and run with it. This is one of the most common ways that a non-believer will argue. A digesting of one word or phrase will change the discussion from a conversation to an argument.

Attendance taker at the meeting of the twelve disciples: "Matt, Bart, Pete, Jimmy, Jimbo, Tom, Johnny, Andy, Phil, Thad, Simon-says, and Hey Jude (real name Thaddeus, not to be confused with Thad and not to be known as Thad 2)."

The rich young ruler was a yardstick.

A Roman spy, seeing how popular Jesus is at the Sermon on the Mount, tries to get a head count: "I, II, III, IV, V, VI, VII..."

Sometimes the clouds backfire. It's not that they don't work, but sparks can happen and make lightening, and immediately following is the loud crash of thunder. It is so cool!

Learning to ride a bike or learning to walk. Once you learn you don't forget how. But, by the same token, if you stop riding and walking for an extended time period, eventually when you do try it again you will be a bit wobbly. And, in the case of the Christian Life, if you never learn, you won't even be able to wobble.

WHERE DO I SIGN UP?

Where do I sign up? How do I know when I have done enough? How does one reach the point when they can say, "I have done enough, it's time to relax and wait until I die; then I will surely get into heaven."? When will I know that I have become the Christian that God expects me to be?

Of the following responses, please select the one that best answers generally the questions above:

1. I know, but I can't tell you, it's a secret.
2. When you are there, you will know it.
3. The answers are blowing in the wind.
4. It depends.
5. None of the above.

The above exchange is what has become known in the education field as the "trick question". When detailing the answers one by one, most of the time you have to go with the famous "none of the above". Some examples of the importance and variance of the answers to these questions follow.

Where do I sign up? Nowhere, the grace and greatness of God is available to all. However, pledging service and support for a church, charities, and outreach to the world are the types of signatures which enable you to aid and assist in ways and to the extent that you never dreamed possible.

How do I know when I have done enough? Never in this life; but a deeply rooted Christian life dedicated to studying the teachings of Jesus, having an understanding of the Holy Spirit, and having an intimate relationship with God, can result in an immediate answer right after death with all the rewards of heaven.

How does one reach the point when they can say, "I have done enough, it's time to relax and wait until I die; then I will surely get into heaven"? The answer is never, you don't retire from being a Christian. Your means of service and support may change, but you continue all facets of your Christian living until you transfer to the next level.

When will I know that I have become the Christian that God expects me to be? Again, never in this life – we should always be striving for the ideal example as represented by the life of Jesus.

How do I surrender to God? How do I know I have the Holy Spirit in me?

We have the manual for following as God has intended for us in the form of the Bible. Jesus is our model for life; it is impossible to attain perfection, but through His sacrifice and resurrection we have the mind and the means to mount the attempt.

As a start, re-read carefully the chapters in John in which Jesus assures the disciples that they can continue what he has started. Chapter 14 is Jesus speaking to the subject of the way to the Father and the promise of the Holy Spirit. In Chapter 15 He uses the vine and the branches illustration. The speaking of Jesus in Chapter 16 details the work of the Holy Spirit (verses 12-15), and tells of the JOY they will be filled with after He leaves them to return to the Father. At the end of chapter 16 are these words: "'You believe at last!' Jesus answered." (Verse 31) He then reveals that at first when He leaves they will be separated, but concludes in verse 33 by telling them "But take heart! I have overcome the world!"

Finally, in chapter 17 (quoting various verses), immediately prior to His arrest, Jesus prays. And Jesus prays for everyone! First He prays for Himself. "Father, the time has come." Then He prays for the disciples. "Now they know that everything You have given Me comes from You." Finally He prays for all believers. "I have given them the glory that You gave Me, that they may be one as We are one: I in them and You in Me."

Fruits of the Spirit

In his letter to the Galatians, Paul spells out the descriptive virtues, or fruit, of the Holy Spirit. "But the Fruit of the Spirit is love, joy, peace, patience, kindness, goodness, faithfulness, gentleness, and self control. Against such things there is no law." (Galatians 5: 22-23)

Immediately prior to the fruit listing is a partial list of the "acts of the sinful nature". (See verses 19-21 for details.) Paul uses his letters in order to keep the faith alive for the Christian followers in various cities and towns while he is locked up in prison. In this section of the Galatians letter, he uses the fruit and the sinful nature listings to stress the importance of honoring God and treating others in the ways that Jesus had taught. We are declared free by Jesus with the Truth, but we must not use our freedom to commit or to justify the acts of sinning.

As Paul states, "The entire law is summed up in a single command: Love your neighbor as yourself." (Galatians 5:14)

How can we improve as Christians?

If you have ever asked yourself this question, many suggestions (answers) can be found in the letters of Paul. Paul uses the letters as his communication from prison in order to keep in contact with the Christian communities he started before he found his way into various prisons. The letters praise, thank, and ask for continued prayers for himself and his associates, as well as expressing his joy at knowing that the work of the Christian body continues in his absence. He then usually goes about telling the people what exactly they should be doing in addition to what is being done. Then too, Paul uses the opportunities of the letters to chastise the followers for the things which his heard that they are not doing and are detrimental to the work at hand. Second Corinthians is an excellent epistle to study in determining what the life of a Christian should consist of and what rewards can be expected for obedience and commitment.

Again, keep in mind that earthly rewards are secondary: heavenly rewards are the primary reason for our lives. One of the greatest lessons of Truth from scripture is from Mark 8:36, when Jesus asks, "What good is it for a man to gain the whole world, yet forfeit his soul?"

When will I know that I have become the Christian that God expects me to be?

Again, you won't know, but here are some points which each individual should consider when determining where the right path leads:

We accept God the Father as omnipotent.

We accept God the Son, Jesus, as the risen Savior who died for us, to take away our sins.

We accept God the Holy Spirit as the driving force in our lives.

We take everything to God, unashamed and repentant, through prayer, service and commitment.

We analyze actions, not by earthly gains, but through considerable thought, prayer, research, and anticipation of consequences according to God. With this process we come to decisions about the right things to do. We are also capable of distinguishing between thoughts and ideas which come to mind as either Christ-like or evil.

We admit our sins, pray for forgiveness, grant forgiveness to others, and educate and prepare ourselves to go and sin no more.

We realize that the Christian Life is a never-ending learning, serving, and earning process.

BUMPER STICKERS
ON THE CLOUDS

You may feel that "Bumper Stickers on the Clouds" uses an odd presentation for God communicating with us, but the following are vital quotes straight from the Gospels. *Don't miss these messages!*

"Do unto others as you would have them do unto you."
(Luke 6: 31)

"For God so loved the world that He gave His one and only Son, that whoever believes in Him shall not perish but have Eternal Life."
(John 3:16)

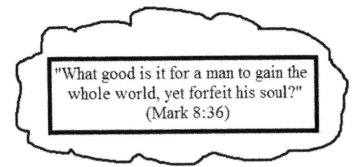

"What good is it for a man to gain the whole world, yet forfeit his soul?"
(Mark 8:36)

"He is not here;
He has risen, just as He said."
(Matthew 28: 6)

"Because you have seen Me, you have believed; blessed are those who have not seen and yet have believed!"
(John 20: 29)

"Love the Lord your God with all your heart and with all your soul and with all your mind."
(Matthew 22:37)

"Therefore go and make disciples of all nations." (Matthew 28: 19)

Here I am! I stand at the door and knock. If any one answers the door, I will come in and eat with him, and he with Me. (Revelation 3: 20)

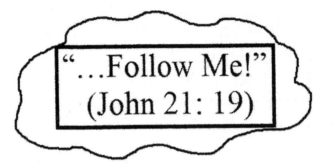

"...Follow Me!"
(John 21: 19)

"I am the way and the truth and
the life. No one comes to the
Father except through Me."
(John 14: 6)

"You cannot serve both
God and money."
(Matthew 6: 24)

"If you believe, you will receive
whatever you ask for in prayer."
(Matthew 21: 22)

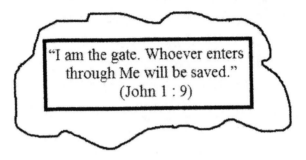

"I am the gate. Whoever enters through Me will be saved."
(John 1 : 9)

"I am not ashamed of the Gospel..." (Romans 1: 16)

"It is more blessed to give
than to receive."
(Acts 20: 35)

"A new command I give you:
Love one another. As I have loved you,
so you must love one another."
(John 13: 34)

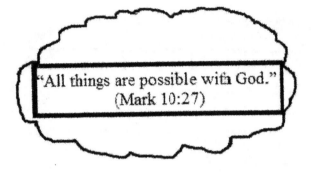

"All things are possible with God."
(Mark 10:27)

"Go into the all the world and preach
the Good News to all creation."
(Mark 16: 15)

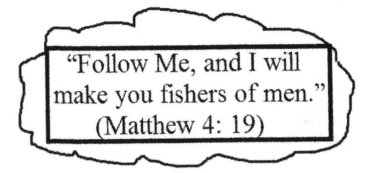

"Follow Me, and I will make you fishers of men."
(Matthew 4: 19)

"And surely I am with you always, to the very end of the age."
(Matthew 28: 20)

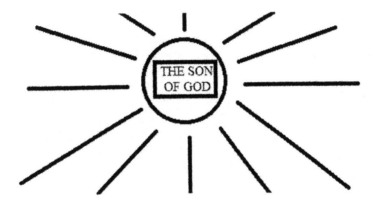